Prayers and Poems of Jack Stevens

A collection of poems, prayers, and songs by Jack Stevens

ISBN 978-1-105-55943-3

Typesetting, editing and formatting by Chris Clark.

Table of Contents

I dedicated this book to my wife Verne, who gives me so much love and patience. And to my Mother who gave me also the love and the upbringing that made me who I am today.

Jack Stevens

Poems

Mama

As I sit here and think of the many times I should have told you just how much I love you, and how you were always there when I needed your loving, soothing voice.

When I was sick or just plain lonely, but for whatever the reason I missed a moment I could have given back the love that was only mine to give.

As my life is in my twilight years, I pray to God in heaven that some day I will be able to tell you, Mama, “I love you”

America the home for me

America is the home for me, land of the redwood tree

Where streams are clear and stars are bright, as they shine throughout the night

The air is fresh the skies are blue, where apples grow and pumpkins too

The fish that swim and the birds that fly, show their love as they pass by

The wheat grows to make my bread; the cotton grows to make my bed

The honey from the flowers bright, all are growing in god’s sight

America is the home for me, where all can grow up free

America, my home

America is the home for me
Land of the redwood tree
With rushing streams and crystal lakes
With mountain high and prairies wide
All beneath the starlit sky
With sage and aspen, pine and oak
And a lot of just plain folk
With wheat that is golden brown
There is enough food to go around
With fish and fowl and cattle too
And with jobs that all can do
America is my home you see
Because my father gave it to me

Thy table

Lord as we come to thy table
May be bring with us our troubles and trials
So that we may share them with you
Only then we can cleanse our souls

Lord as we come to the table,
May we bring with us our hopes and dreams,
Asking for your guidance
For only then will we be able to bring them to fulfillment

Lord as we come to thy table,

May we bring with us our love of one another

Sharing with you a small part of the glory of what life is about

Lord as we come to thy table,

May we bring with us the knowledge that through your sacrifices,

We may share with our father the hope that through you we can have eternal life

My country

July 10, 2011

My country 'tis of thee, sweet land of liberty, we thank you most holy God, for this land, we call home.

Where are all free to worship you where ever, when ever and however we wish.

We thank you father for heroes brave and true who have carried this torch of freedom to the four corners of the earth. Most holy God please keep this land we love always free and may our song always be, “God bless America”.

Night stars

God sent for all to see, the beauty of the growing tree

The ocean swells, and skies so blue, lets you know he loves you too

The gentle wind and summer rain brings us love from our king

The love we share, the joy and pain fills us all with life again

The beauty of God

The beauty of my god to see

The flowing wind through the tall oak tree

To feel the soft summers breeze

To watch the birds glide though the sky

As the sun goes by

To hear the crickets on a fine spring eve

To feel the raindrops from the sky

To watch the waters go rushing by

The cactus in the desert sea

Reminds me of what should be

America

God made America so shiny bright

He gave it stars to light the night

And mountains, valleys, rivers, streams

Which feeds its life and fulfills its dreams

The beauties there for all to see

What God has given to you and me

Oh the glory of our land may for freedom it ever stands

Thank you father up above for this land we dearly love

America's beauty is thrilling to see

From ocean to ocean it pleases me

The rocky crags, the running streams

The valley floor where all is green

The desert with air so clear

You have to know that God lives here

Rain

Sept 20, 2009

Mountain high and rushing springs

Fill the earth with life again

Fish will swim and birds will sing

All because of the summer rain

Grass will grow on the land below

Because god made it so

The sky so blue the stars so bright

Guides us through another night

Verne and I

Verne and I wrote this together on the road in the 1980's.

Did you take time today to take a moment to pray?

Did you take time today to talk to someone along the way?

Did you take time today to watch the children as they play?

Did you take time today to hear the voice of one so dear

Did you take time today to enjoy the smell of new mowed hay?

Did you take time today to feel the warmth of the sun

Did you take time tonight to see the stars so shiny and bright?

Did you take time tonight to thank God for all that's right?

Did you take time tonight for all the blessings up above?

Did you take time?

Sunlight

Written March 2008

Sunlight on the morning dew

Brings God's love to me and you

The song birds sing with good cheer

Yes they know that spring is here

The grass is fast becoming green
The lord has shown his love again
The squirrels all run and play in the warmth of the day

The flowers of the early spring
Bring God’s love to us again
Yellows, purples, reds, and greens
Let us know its spring again

Popcorn and peanuts

Jan 1, 2009

America the land of popcorn and peanuts
Land of old age pensions and working men
Land of million dollar homes and homeless shacks
Land of raging waters and clear blue skies
Land of honey bees and Brussels sprouts
Land of history books and comic strips
Land of motorcycles and pickup trucks
Land of pine trees and cheddar cheese
Where there are people like you and me
Who give a smile to all they meet

Love

Roses are red the sky is blue
Posies are purple and I love you
Robins sing and hummingbirds fly
Life is full of joy for you and I
Morning comes with all its dew
Let me show my love for you
Honey is sweet and water melons too
Apples are juicy and I love you
Bells ring and children sing
Your touch is as gentle as summer rain
This I know my love is true
And I want no one but you

Sweet kindness

Tender baby lying in straw
Sent from heaven to love us all
Bringing good will near and far
Showering God's mercy to us all
Blessed Jesus from above
God's sweet kindness wrapped in love

Coming home

Across the fields of golden grain, mountain peaks, and rushing streams

Prairies wide and dark grey skies, falls to earth the summer rain

We say goodbye to one more spring, coyotes howl and bees that sting

It’s so good to be home again

The stars at night are shining bright, another one of God’s delights

Family and friends we greet

Once more with love and kindness at our door

It’s so good to be home again

Message

Sept 25, 2009

Light from heaven shines so bright

It lights the earth both day and night

It sends a message for all to see

That god loves both you and me

It guides us through another day

As we travel along life’s long highway

It warms the earth so food can grow

It melts the snow so streams may flow

Cowboys

October 29, 2010

The sun is shining
The grass is green
The birds are singing
It must be spring
The flowers are blooming
On yonder hill
Butterflies flying
With colors bright
The cowboys riding
The open range
The wolves are howling
For the summers rain
The crops are planted
There's no frost anywhere
The children are playing
In the city streets
The sound of laughter is so sweet
There's life again
In the village square
The sun is shining everywhere

Gifts

December 4, 2009

God made the earth, the land, and the sea
The waters and fruit from the tree
He made it all for you and me

God made the heavens, the sun and the moon
The stars and the planets and asteroids too
He made it all for you and me

God made the water, rivers, and streams
Snow on the mountains and flowers in spring
He made it all for you and me

Life's highway

March 18, 2010

Lord, as we travel down life’s highway and as we face each new day, may our prayer be that each footstep will guide us on the path of love. We know that our way will not always be filled with sunshine but with your light we will never be lost. I’m tired, it’s been a long day, but Jesus has been with me along the way. He’s led me to this place of rest, from this long, long day. Tomorrow as I start another day he will guide my journey yet another day.

America reprise

America, what a wonderful place to call home
From the highest mountain to the lowest valley
From sea to sea, border to border
Rivers and streams with sun and rain
Which refreshes the earth and fields of green
Where God's love is everywhere
In flowers and trees and gentle breeze
And the beauty of music from birds that sing
America, what a wonderful place that God gave me

Bright stars

Holy night, stars so bright
Guide the shepherds on that cold winter night
To a manger where he lay
The savior was born on a bed of hay

Holy night the angels sing
Glory to the newborn king
Sent from heaven to the earth below
To help the children as they grow

Gods grace

Lord, through your grace we have life

Life to be free to enjoy the beauty of the setting sun

the beauty of a child at play

The beauty of the morning bright

The beauty of the stars at night

The beauty of a loved one dear

The beauty of the ear to hear, the music that's so soft and clear

Village square

Green is the grass in the village square

The old people gather there, telling stories of their years gone by

Enjoying the sunshine of their golden years

The live oak tree stands mighty tall

It will have acorns coming this fall

The children run and play in the sunshine all the day

The lovers are there at night

Talking love by the moonlight

Oh, if only it could be someone like you and me

Green is the grass in the village square

How I wish that we were there

Remembering heroes

Today I walked where heroes lay

Beneath a mound of cold red clay

They fought and died

So we could live in freedom

God bless these heroes where they lay

Beneath a mound of cold red clay

Today I walked on a mountain high where many good men fought and died

Today as I kneel and pray I thank God for those who lie beneath the cold red clay

The spoken word

Dawn breaks so bright and clear

It lets you know that God is near

The sun, with its warming rays

Burst forth with it a new born day

The sounds of life can be heard

The glory of the spoken word

The smell of the fresh cut hay

The laughter as the children play

The beauty of the plants so bright

Lets you know that all is right

The blossoms on the apple trees

The humming of the honey bee

The clouds that float across the sky

The glory that god gave you and I

Standing on the Mountain

Standing on the mountain, looking down below
I can see the beauty of nature unfold
I can hear birds and rushing streams
I can smell the flowers and the coming rain
I can feel the wind as it gently blows
Pushing the clouds like cones of snow

Work

We plant the plants and sow the seeds
We water the garden all with ease
We pick the fruit and rake the leaves
Leaving the work to whom we please
We go to work and stay all day
Only wanting just our pay
All the work they should take away
We laugh and play the live long day
Hurting those that get in our way
Poking fun and jeers at those
Whose ideas that we oppose
All of the above we know is true
But just tell me it isn't true
This I command you to do
Seeing you would make me blue

Eyes

God gave me eyes to see the beauty of the growing tree

He gave me hands to feel the wood, in hopes I'd use it as I should

The fruit from the apple tree, keeps me healthy as can be

The leaves with their shades of green

Makes me feel so fresh and clean

The branches that reach so high

Look like they might touch the sky

All my life I will understand

God made the trees as a gift to man

Spread the word

God gave us voices to sing, all the praises of the living king

To tell of his wondrous love and his promises from above

As a choir, our prayer will be, make us worthy of trust from thee

God gave us eyes to see, all the wonders of life

May we see what the dear father would have us be

Our voices will be clear, give us harmony as we sing for thee

God gave us love to be, all the family of Christ you see

Always sharing concern and joy, help us make our voices clear

Spreading love both far and near

Jesus Christ the chosen one, both the father and the son

Thanks God

I thank you God for songs I sing

I thank you for the joy they bring

I thank you both for day and night

I thank you for loves pure light

I thank you god for eyes that see

The beauty of the chestnut tree

I thank you for the summer rain

And for the fields full of golden grain

I thank you God for colors bright

I thank you for the stars at night

The joys in winter

Guiding light, stars bright

Gives us hope on a cold winter night

Angels sing church bells ring

Oh the joy this season brings

Joys in the day

Brush your teeth, comb your hair
Go outside and breathe the air
Feel the warmth of the newborn day
Watch the children as they play
Thank the lord for one and all
For the short and for the tall

Watch the birds in the sky
As they soar, as they fly
Beauty to all, they bring, in the early morning spring
Hear the lark and the whippoorwill
As they sing the music of the lord
That the bluebird brings

Home tonight

The road is long the deserts wide
The mountains reach up to the sky
The flowers bloom coyotes sing
The earth is wet with summer rain
The rivers deep the stars so bright
God has brought us home tonight

Our savior

Jesus Christ the prince of glory

Jesus Christ the holy son

He was sent to save the people

He was sent to take them home

Jesus Christ the lord of mercy

Jesus Christ the gentle one

Jesus Christ the king of heaven

Jesus Christ the chosen one

He was born of the Virgin Mary

Given by the love of God

Jesus Christ the holy savior

Sent from God the three in one

Mercy is his gift, free to everyone

Time for rest

Sometimes when we get to busy we don't leave time for rest. But then the Lord in all his glory, he knows what is best, slows down a function of our body, causing us to pause, now we have time for resting, thanks to God our savior who made us all.

If we use this time of resting to focus on what we have been doing, we will find that the most important thing in our lives we have neglected. God gave us our minds and bodies to bring forth the beauty of his creation. We must remember that after six days God rested and as he rested he looked and saw what he had worked for was good.

Giving

Why do I give? Do I give because it's expected of me? Do I give because it makes me feel good? Do I give because it's the right thing to do? Let's hope that all of the above are reasons that I give. From the beginning, God gave, and by giving I am here today. God, the giver of life, I pray that you take me through another day. Let me see the birds that fly as I search that clear blue sky. May I feel the warmth of day, may I hear the children play. Could I have another day, to thank you lord, in this I pray. What do I give? I give my time and love which are the most important things God has given to me.

Worthy

Lord as I come to thy table as I kneel at the cross may I see

The glory of thy salvation and the new life it brings to me

Lord as I come to thy table and confess all my sins

May I be a child of thy kingdom and a witness for all to see

Lord as I pray at thy table and receive thy many blessings

May I be worthy of thy kindness and serve no one but thee

People

Verne Jean

Dedicated to my wife.

My little girl, her name is Verne Jean

She can be pretty, she can be mean

She can be forward, she can be shy

And that’s why she’s the apple of my eye

Our life together has its ups and downs

But it is the best life that can be found

For sixteen years she’s been my mate

There is nothing better, this side of heaven’s gate

I love you V.J. with all my heart

You will be mine till death do us part

Sister

Dedicated to Margarite.

My sister M, she was so sweet she made me happy each time we’d meet

Quick to praise, slow to scorn, god made an angel the day she was born

Her life was full, this I know, because her children told me so

Shes gone to heaven, she’s at rest, with the man she loved the best

Brother

Dedicated to Al.

My brother Al, god rest his soul
He gave me more love than can ever be told
He showed me strength when I was a child
He gave me hope when I was wild
He taught me to stand straight and tall
To get back up when I had a fall

My brother Al, he's gone to rest
With his lord whom he loved best
To his home in heaven high
Where I will meet him when I die
Because Al taught me to love and obey
my sweet Jesus who will lead the way

Window pane

Dedicated to Myrtle Waugh

Window Pane, oh so bright, holds the stars that shine at night

Frames the children as they play, mirrors love as families pray

Makes the day so very bright, as it gives off loves pure light

Reflects the moon and heavens above, and speaks to us of God's pure love

Sparrows, Blue Jays, hummingbirds too, come to feed within my view

God has made his world so fair, and through my window pane I can share

Good Bye

In memory of Max Crestetto

Jesus came the other day

He came and took my friend away

He took him to his home on high

Where he will stay in the by–and-by

I'm sure if we could hear him, Max would say

Don't be weeping for this bit of clay

Because I'm with my father this fine day

I love you all but it's time to say

My Lord has called, so I'm on my way

Bill

Sometimes in the evening when the wind is still

I hear someone calling, it must be Bill

Asking me why Saigon fell

And why he died in that living hell

The answer to that I do not know

I just hope that history will show

He died for freedom in that far off land

Not just for some stupid master plan

Robert T

In memory of Robert Tenant.

We've all heard church mice dear

Hurrying around both far and near

One thing at TTUMC we don't have one in Bobby T

What we have is what you see

He does his work with such great cheer

His knowledge of how things work is uncanny clear

With a twinkle in his eye , he makes it look as simple as apple pie

Oh I wish that I could be half the man as Robert T

Christ Jesus

He gives us flowers and the rain

He makes the pretty robins sing

He shares with us the joy and pain

He teaches us to love again

Jesus Christ the gentle one, Jesus Christ the good lords son

God in heaven, up above touch us with thy gentle hand

Make us all a better man

Teach us all truth and faith

Give us courage to face the day

Who am I?

Who am I?

I am a father, grandfather, and a great-grand papa

All of which I am most proud of

I am a believer of the living God

Who gave me all that I am and ever will be

I am a proud member of the armed forces of The United States

A law abiding citizen, willing to defend the land with my life

This is who I am

Prayers

Prayers of the heart

Feb 1, 2008

Our father which art in heaven to whom we sing, how great thou are. If only we believe and live by these simple words, they will take us all to heaven some sweet day. There we will stand in the presence of our mighty king. We will join the heavenly chorus as we sing holy, holy, holy God, to whom all glory and honor be yours now and forever shall be. What a wonderful time that will be where all will abide forever more, in our eternal home, among Gods angels rejoicing in the knowledge that there will be no war, hunger, anger, sickness or sorrow, but only peace and good will to all. We will feast at the table with Jesus and the army of God. Thank you father for giving all who will trust and obey your holy word, a place at your table

Pray of hope

Whom do I seek when I am tired, who gives me hope when I am low

Who helps me through the lonely night, and brings with morning the suns warm glow

Who gives me flowers in the spring and children’s voices as they sing of the praises of our king

God in heaven up above, teach us all thy tender love

Gift to the world

As God gave Mary our lord and savior, she in turn gave him to the world. The world that today is in need of his guiding hand and thoughtful word of love. If we take this need with us as we return to our homes tonight, we will find how blessed we that live in this land of the free are. To you, to all blessings flow, we give thanks

Amen

Table prayer

Today Lord, as we come to your table we give you thanks for the many blessings that you shower upon us daily. We humble ask that through your love, we as a family will grow in the ways that you would have us to be. We thank you lord for the warmth of the sun and the beauty of the day. To you whom glory and honor belong, Amen

Meal grace

Lord, this food we share with one another, we know is a gift, given through the love that you give. We thank you for the ones we share your gift with. We pray that each of us will be forever grateful for our daily bread. In your name we pray

Amen

Coming home

God through this night, as we return to our homes, we are thankful for our time in service and our safe return. We know that through your mercy we have a place to call home. Please watch over those whose time is now to guard our freedom

To you we pray, Amen

Prayer for heroes

Most loving God,

May our prayer be that the brave men and women of our armed forces be fortified in the knowledge that in their trust is placed the continued freedom of our beloved America. May our honored dead be not forgotten and may we accept the torch of freedom that is ours to hold high. To you, all glory and honor.

Prayer of thanks for the world

Heavenly Father

We can only realize the magnitude of your love when we see the snow covered mountains or the valleys, deserts, rushing waters, clear blue skies, and stars at night, redwood trees and grass so green, the fish that swim and birds that sing, rows of corn and golden grain, the smell of roses, and gentle rain, the voices of loved ones dear. These gifts from you let us know that you are always near.

Prayer of the American Legion

All mighty and merciful God, we are so grateful for the opportunity to pay tribute to the thousands of men and women who died in the service of our country who now lay in your hollow ground, and beneath your rolling seas. We thank you Father for this free land and the different races and religions that call America home. We pray Lord, that as a nation we will always be willing to sacrifice all that we have and are, to protect our home and what it stands for.

To you our loving God, all glory and honor, Amen

Veterans

In this place Lord, we come together to share a common bond with each other, a bond that only Veterans may understand. We thank you for this day that you have given us to enjoy with love for our families and friends. We ask you, who is all powerful, to guard over those that we have placed in harm's way, to please bring them back home safe and sound when their duties are complete.

We ask this in your holy name, Amen

Prayer of purpose

Lord, we sometimes wonder why you gave us life and what you would have us do with it. Then along comes a person in need or a task that we are best suited for. That's when you whisper, "for this moment I gave you life". Most Holy Father, please forgive us when we don't accept your call as you would have us to do. Please help us to love our fellow man and please watch over our troops as they protect our way of life. To you, who gave us life, we pray, Amen.

Life's highway prayer

Lord, as we travel down life's highway and we face each new day, may our prayer be a prayer of thanksgiving. Thank you for the guidance and love that you give with each footstep we take. We know Father that our way will not always be filled with sunshine, but with your light, we will never be lost. As we return to our homes tonight, may we bring peace and love to our loved ones.

To you we pray, Amen

Love and friendship

Most gracious God, we gather here to share our love and friendship with each other. We walk today for our brothers and sisters who are less fortunate.

We know Lord, that as we give our time, energy, and resources, we are giving

back a small portion of the many blessings that you give us.

May we walk with a song of praise in our hearts and joy in our steps, free from pain.

To you from whom all blessings flow, we glorify your holy name.

Old year

The old year is fading fast, the new one is just beginning. Lord, we look forward to the challenges of what God will set before us. Please help us to understand and accomplish these things. We ask you Father, to forgive the many sins of the past year and guide our footsteps as we walk the walk and talk the talk of the new year. Lord, we ask you to accept into your arms, everyone that will be called home this year. We thank you for our country and for the many who continue to keep our home safe. All glory and honor be yours, Amen.

Hope

We ask you Lord, to guide the American Nation to be a light that will be the hope of all mankind. We thank you Father for the love we share with our families, our fellow Veterans, and all Americans. To those who are carrying the torch of freedom around the world, we pray that you will keep them safe and bring them back home to their loved ones.

To you, the light of the world we pray , Amen.

Comrades prayer

Tonight as we gather in this place, let us remember the many comrades who came before us. We know that you have made it possible that when we were called to duty in the service of our beloved America, that through your love we are still here tonight. Please watch over our fellow veterans and the brave ones on active duty. To all honor and glory be yours for everyone, Amen.

Prayer of gladness

Lord, as we come to you with gladness in our hearts, with the knowledge that we have the freedom to assemble here as free man to conduct the business that will come before us tonight, let us never forget the daily gifts that only you can give. We thank you most gracious God for the brave men and women of our armed forces. May they know that they are loved and respected for what they are doing to keep this nation free. Please watch over them tonight and bring them home safely. In your name we pray Amen.

Prayer for family

Lord as we celebrate this holiday season with family and friends and all the good cheer, let us not forget that all of this is given to us through the love that you so freely give. For the many who are serving in harms way, we ask that your light of hope help them to know that they are loved and will be greatly missed. To you whom all glory and honor belong. Amen

New Years prayer

Grant us our most Holy God for this most holy time of the year, to show our love to our fellow man by words, deeds, and cheer. May we keep Jesus in our hearts and that we follow his commandment to do unto others as we would have them do unto us. As this year comes to a close, we pray that the New Year will bring peace on earth and good will to all mankind and our love and respect will be our way this coming year. Please keep your light shinning and guide our footsteps now and forever. Amen

Spring

As the cold of winter fades and the beauty of spring bursts forth from your good earth, we thank you for your gifts of love. If we pause from our daily lives and look around life would be full of love. Most Holy Father, we ask that you protect those that have been placed in harm's way and may we Americans show the world hope is to be an instrument of your peace. To you all glory and love we pray Amen.

Easter

Lord as we celebrate the time of your resurrection may we never forget the love of our holy father for us that through the death of his only son we are able to be forgiven for our sins. May our nation always be a beacon of your love and a hope to the world. In your name we pray, Amen

Summer prayer

Most heavenly father,

We thank you for the summer rain and the fields of golden grain. We thank you for what we planted this last spring, now it's harvest time again. May we see all that we have gained, to share the love and relieve the pain that hunger brings. When the cold of the winter is through, let us start fresh and new

July 4th

Lord as we celebrate the anniversary of the birth of our nation, we thank you for the leaders that have answered the call to guide us through both good and bad times. We know Lord that you have allowed us to be a land where people are free to be whatever they wish to be if they only apply themselves. Most loving God, we thank you for the beauty of our homeland and to you who gives it life.

Veterans day

As we celebrate this time of remembrance, let us not forget those who have gone to that final resting place in God's kingdom. May we never forget the sacrifices of those left on the many battlefields, so the living can enjoy the freedoms that this great nation affords. To we whom the torch of freedom has been passed may we forever hold it high. We give thanks in your name Amen.

Crop walk prayer

Sept 2010

The crop walk in Alameda is held every year in or near October. Crop walks are held at other locations too, for more information see http://www.crophungerwalks.org/alameda/

Most gracious God we gather here to share the love and friendship with each other.

Lord we walk today for our brothers and sisters who are less fortunate.

We know Lord that as we give of our time, energy, and resources we are giving back a small portion of the many blessings you give is.

Father may we walk with a song of praise in our heart and joy in our steps free from pain.

To you from whom all blessings flow we glorify you Holy name. Amen.

Prayer for Thanksgiving 1

Holy Father, as we celebrate the season of Thanksgiving in this free land and the bountiful gifts that you provide us, please show us the path that you would have us to follow, bring us the leadership and love to all of your children throughout the world. Loving God, may we never forget the price payed by those who fought and died for our land. Please watch over our loved ones who are on the front lines of freedom. To you whose love is forever, we pray in your name Amen.

Prayer for Thanksgiving 2

Too often father we take for granted the many blessings you bestow upon us. That all we have and ever will have is given to us with a love that is only yours to give. Tomorrow we celebrate our national day of Thanksgiving. May we keep in mind as we enjoy this day and meal, the many people that will be without. Our prayer is that someday all will be able to enjoy this blessed day. Watch over our service persons and keep them safe from harm. To you be all honor and glory Amen.

Happy Birthday

Today Lord as we wait the coming of the Christ child, we give thanks for the hope that someday we will truly say peace on earth to all mankind. The love that is Christmas is a celebration that brings out the goodness in all that only our God can give. It is my prayer that the ones who are guarding our homeland will be comforted in the knowledge that they will be missed during this holiday season. To you the Christ child we say happy birthday

The gift of giving

Most Gracious and loving father, we thank you for the gift of giving which you gave to us, the gift of yourself in the birth of your son. Father, this holiday season may all of the prayers be that of peace on earth and good will towards all men be spoken with true meaning and may love conquer the hate and mistrust this coming year. In your most holy name we pray Amen.

Christmas prayer

O holy night, the angels sang, the world is blessed with a newborn king.

We thank you heavenly father for the most precious of all, the gift of your only begotten son, our risen lord.

During this time of Christmas, please God help the ones who are guarding our shores, to know that they are loved and that they will be in our hopes and prayers.

We pray lord that with the new year mankind will find peace on earth and good will to all

Amen

End of year prayer

We thank you most Holy God for the love that you have given us this year. We know that without your love life would cease to have meaning. To those who have been called home this year, we thank you for the time they spent with us and we humbly ask you to forgive them for their sins and welcome them into your kingdom. To those of us that you have granted the time we have left on our life's journey, please guide us as we travel down our paths to our final home. Amen.

Prayer for those on duty

Dear Lord, as we come to the end of another day let us reflect on the many blessings you give us. Sometimes in our hurried days we forget that through your love we receive all we have and will ever have. To those who we as a nation have placed in harm's way, please watch over them and may they feel loved and honored. To you whom all praise and glory belong, in your name we pray Amen.

Another thanks

Lord, help me this day I pray to hear the children as they play

To feel the warmth of the summer breeze, to see the birds in the trees

To love those that I hold dear and forgive those that I fear

To walk each day with head held high, because I know that you're close by

Lord, help me this day I pray to help my fellow man along the way

To show love from my heart and to help them build a better start

To build a place of peace and quiet where rest and love can bring new hope

To those who have the joy of knowing you to keep them afloat

Prayer of love and friendship

Most gracious and loving father, we thank you for the friendship and love that all of us share in the spirit of competition. We ask you lord to be with each athlete as they test their skills, please watch over them and keep them from harm. We thank you lord for our homeland and the freedom we have to be whatever we strive to be. To you all glory and honor to our risen Lord, we pray Amen.

Old Glory

September 23rd 2011

This flag called old glory is the living symbol of this land of freedom called America. With its stars of white on a blue background supported by the stripes of red and white, makes me feel so thankful that I live under it. The red stripes represent the blood, sweat and tears, the white stripes for the purity for which it stands and the land inside the two oceans and clear blue skies. This flag called old glory is my flag, how about you?

Flag pole dedication

This was written for a dedication in San Jose, CA August 19th 2011 at a center for the homeless, both veterans and non-veterans.

We dedicate this flag and flagpole to all who are serving, have served and will some day serve in the armed forces of this country, our homeland the United States of America.

May all who pass by feel the love and hope this places offers to all.

To those who have donated their time and or resources to make this dedication possible, many thanks.

We praise God to whom we give all glory and honor for this free country that is given us.

Thank you.

The old lady

January 30, 2011

What a beautiful old lady I saw today.

She was wrinkled, faded, frayed and torn.

To be over two hundred years young she is still the most loved and honored of all, my flag Old Glory.

What a magnificent gift God gave to all who love the freedoms that this beautiful lady represents, the red, white and blue my flag Old Glory.

For the red blood that has been shed to protect, the white for the purity and the deep blue for the love of the nation, again we thank God for my flag Old Glory.

Songs

Communion song

Lord as I come to thy table

As I bow on bended knee

As I take of thy blessings

I know all good things come from thee

And may I always remember the love you gave to me

Blessed forever my Jesus, I love thee

Lord as I pray at thy table

May sins be forgiven of me

As I take of thy blessings

I know you gave life for me

And may I always remember the love you gave to me

Blessed forever my Jesus, I love thee

Crop walk

Walk for the hungry, walk for the hungry, we walk for the hungry today

Lord show us the way to have mercy, we pray as we walk for the hungry today

Walk for the hungry, walk for the hungry, we walk for the hungry today

There are millions today who can't pay their way, so please walk for the hungry today

Walk for the hungry, walk for the hungry, we walk for the hungry today

Lord give us the strength to walk all the way, as we walk for the hungry today

Walk for the hungry, walk for the hungry, we walk for the hungry today

We who have more lets share with the poor as we walk for the hungry today

Take my hand

June 8, 1981

When the world seems so grey, and my life from day to day is so dreary and long, if I only turn to thee, then my worries will be set free, if only I take your hand.

Take my hand every day, take my hand all the way, take my hand precious lord, take my hand.

When the clouds of doubt appear and my mind is far from clear. You will always be near if only I trust in you. Then your love will see me through if only I take you hand.

Take my hand every day, take my hand all the way, take my hand precious lord, take my hand.

When the time of life is through and I can turn to no one but you, as heavens gates open wide, with you my savior by my side, I will bless thee ever more, take my hand.

Take my hand every day, take my hand all the way, take my hand precious lord, take my hand.

Take my hand when I pray, take my hand when I play, lead me lord in thy ways, take my hand at work each day, take my hand all the way.

Take my hand every day, take my hand all the way, take my hand precious lord, take my hand.

Take my hand every day, take my hand all the way, lead me home, don't let me stray, keep me on the narrow way, take my hand precious Lord take my hand.

Take my hand every day, take my hand all the way, take my hand precious lord, take my hand.

Take my mind every day, this my lord is what I pray, let me prove to all who will that your love is always real, take my mind precious lord take my mind

Take my hand every day, take my hand all the way, take my hand precious lord, take my hand.

Take my life every day, guide my steps along the way, keep me strong in my love for you, in each and every thing I do take my life precious Lord take my life.

Take my hand every day, take my hand all the way, take my hand precious lord, take my hand.

Thank you

August 25, 2009

Thank you for the stars at night.

Thank you for the city lights.

Thank you for the food I eat.

Thank you for the folks I meet.

Thank you for the rising sun.
Thank you for the work thats done.

Thank you for your tender love.
Thank you for your home above.

Thank you for the morning bright.
Thank you for the rain at night.

Thank you for the birds that sing.
Thank you for the rushing stream.

Thank you for love thats true.
Thank you for the oceans blue.